It's getting hot in here!

Jeff, Drew, Justin, and Nick are the melodic masters in 98 Degrees, the hottest band on the airwaves! Find out how four guys from Ohio moved to Los Angeles and formed the group . . . what it was like to record a song with Stevie Wonder . . . and what they did to earn money before they hit it big.

What was life like growing up for brothers Nick and Drew? How did 98 Degrees win a recording contract from the legendary Motown label? What do these hotties look for in a girl? You'll find all the details about the band that makes your temperature rise in . . .

98°

And Rising to the Top!

Look for other celebrity biographies from
Archway Paperbacks

98° and rising to the top!

Nancy Krulik

AN ARCHWAY PAPERBACK Original

AN ARCHWAY PAPERBACK
Published by POCKET BOOKS
New York London Toronto Sydney Tokyo Singapore

AN ARCHWAY PAPERBACK *Original*

An Archway Paperback published by
POCKET BOOKS, a division of Simon & Schuster Inc.
1230 Avenue of the Americas, New York, NY 10020

Copyright © 1999 by Nancy Krulik

ISBN: 0-671-03676-9

First Archway Paperback printing April 1999

10 9 8 7 6 5 4 3 2 1

AN ARCHWAY PAPERBACK and colophon are
registered trademarks of Simon & Schuster Inc.

Front cover photo courtesy of London Features
Insert photos courtesy of Anthony Cutajar/London Features

Printed in the U.S.A.

IL 4+

For Danny, who still gives me fever!

Contents

Contents

98° *and rising to the top!*

From Invisible Men to Hometown Heroes

From the moment Nick Lachey stepped onto the stage at Cincinnati's School for Creative and Performing Arts in August of 1998, he knew something was different. The last time Nick, his brother Drew, and his pal Justin Jeffre had been on that stage they had been students at the school, performing in musicals and dreaming of world-wide stardom.

But that was five years before. Now their schoolboy dreams were on the verge of coming true. Nick, Drew, Justin, and their friend Jeff Timmons were part of a singing group called 98 Degrees. In the past year, the guys had accomplished a lot. They'd scored a recording deal with Motown Records, one of the most respected labels in the industry. They'd already had a hit single ("Invisible Man") which reached number twelve on the *Billboard* charts and went gold. They'd caused a sensation in Europe and Asia, and were just about to release their second CD.

They were also living in New York City, far from their Ohio roots. So why come all the way home to rehearse?

"It makes sense to come back and rehearse for the new show and the new album here," Nick told a reporter from his hometown paper, the *Cincinnati Enquirer*. "In New York, you pay all kinds of big money for a rehearsal hall. Besides, Ohio's where we're from. It definitely feels good."

Coming home had a calming effect on Jeff, Justin, Nick, and Drew. And that was something they desperately needed. The past year had brought a lot of excitement into the lives of these four Ohio hunks. When the guys were in Canada, the crowds of screaming girls were so intense that their concerts made the evening news. And during their late 1997 to early 1998 tour of Asia, it was virtually impossible for Nick, Drew, Jeff, and Justin to make public appearances without security guards flocking around them. One time the guys actually tried putting on fake moustaches and wigs so they could tour around on their own—but the fans sniffed them out right away!

Not that the guys were complaining. They really loved all that fan-demonium! "You get off the plane and you kind of have jet lag and you kind of move slow, and then you get bombarded by fans and it wakes you up! They really give you a lot of energy!" Jeff exclaimed to a reporter for a Malaysian newspaper.

But now the guys were back in their hometown, and they were able to walk the streets with no security at all. They could head down the street to the local grocery store and no one would even so much as glance at them.

How could that be?

Well, like many up-and-coming bands, 98 Degrees had spent a lot of time overseas promoting their debut album, *98 Degrees*. Their concerts in Europe, Asia, and Canada were huge successes, but those shows were a warm-up for what many in the music biz consider to be the toughest market of all—the United States. So even though the guys had gotten a lot of U.S. radio play with "Invisible Man," they only had a small following in the United States.

"Life at home hasn't changed at all," Drew said at the time. "You still gotta take out the trash; you still gotta mow the lawn. A lot of our friends at first, at least mine, were expecting me to change. But I think they realize that I'm the same person."

The guys in 98 Degrees couldn't have known it back then, but their peaceful anonymity was about to come to an end. As the guys spent the dog days of summer sweating through rehearsals in their old high school auditorium in Cincinnati, the Motown hit-making masters were already hard at work in New York, pumping out press releases trumpeting the success of 98 Degrees' newest song, "True to Your Heart." (The guys had recently recorded the song with Motown legend Stevie Wonder as part of the soundtrack for the Disney movie *Mulan.*) Motown was also planning a huge push for the guys' next single, "Because Of You," which would be taken from their upcoming second CD, *98 Degrees and Rising.* There were also plans in the works for major tours of Asia, the U.S., and Canada, which would put the guys on the road in November, and keep them moving throughout the spring of 1999.

But back in August of '98 there was no way Nick and his pals could have known what surprises the last few months of the year would hold for them.

But we sure know now. In the fall of 1998, 98 Degrees released a breakthrough sophomore album that yielded a top five platinum single, and sent their careers into the stratosphere. By the time the clock struck twelve on New Year's Eve, Nick, Drew, Justin, and Jeff were bonafide superstars with more fans than they ever could have imagined.

1998 was definitely the year America discovered what the rest of the world already knew—that 98 Degrees was quite possibly the most exciting group on the pop music scene. But if Jeff, Justin, Nick, and Drew have anything to say about things, 1999 is going be the group's most exciting year yet. The temperature in the music business is rising to a sweltering 98 Degrees.

This is their story.

Success? "Come and Get It!"

To truly follow the 98 Degrees success story you'd need a map of the United States. Here's why: The guys got together as a group in Los Angeles. Their record label, Motown, is named for Detroit, but the company's headquarters are in New York. New York is also where all four guys make their home these days, although their tours have taken them all over the continental U.S. and Hawaii (not to mention Europe, Canada, and Asia).

But if you want to know where the 98 Degrees heat wave really began, you'd have to point your compass toward Ohio. That's the state where Jeff, Justin, Nick, and Drew grew up.

While growing up in Ohio, the 98 Degrees guys had many musical influences. Jeff sang in his school choir. Nick and Drew appeared in high school musicals like *Annie* and *A Christmas Carol.* For a while Justin and Nick sang with a barbershop quartet, and a country-and-western band! The guys all sang pop songs and some oldies too. But their true musical tastes really ran toward rhythm and blues. Especially the classic R&B artists like Stevie Wonder and Marvin Gaye.

The guys in 98 Degrees have always been proud of their Ohio heritage. In fact Drew lists Cleveland as one of his favorite concert spots. But let's face it. If you want to have a music career in the United States, there are only two places where you can start out— New York and Los Angeles.

In 1995, Jeff Timmons was a student at Kent State University in Ohio. Suddenly he decided to quit school and take his chances with a music career. So he loaded up his truck and moved to Beverly. (Okay, so that's what TV's the Beverly Hillbillies did. Jeff actually took a car and moved to a much less prestigious area of Los Angeles, in the hopes of becoming an R&B sensation.)

Jeff went out to California with three friends from Ohio. They had put together a band called Just Us. The members of Just Us tried to get singing gigs in the L.A. area, but mostly they found themselves doing odd jobs around the city trying to make ends meet. Before long, the other band members bailed out. They couldn't take the pressure.

But Jeff was determined to make a go of it.

"What I did after [the group split up] is I went looking for people to sing in the group. I went through all these ads and I couldn't find the right people," Jeff remembers.

Then Jeff ran into John Lipman, someone he knew from Ohio. John agreed to sing with Jeff, and he also recommended two of his friends from Cincinnati's School for Creative and Performing Arts—Nick Lachey and Justin Jeffre. John called his buds right away, and although both Nick and Justin were heavily involved in college studies, they packed their bags and headed out to Los Angeles in search of fame and fortune.

It wouldn't be fair to say that Jeff, Nick,

and Justin's families thought the guys were insane to quit school and move out to California. But their folks *were* a little fearful. After all, Los Angeles can be a nasty town. And the music world isn't exactly known for its kind treatment of young hopefuls. The music biz is more like a fire-breathing dragon that swallows up aspiring musicians and then spits them out like dirt.

"I think my mom was a little skeptical in the beginning," Nick recalls. "But even when [she] didn't agree with what we were doing, she still backed us up. Now I think our moms are our biggest fans. My mom's even in charge of the fan club!"

Finding places to practice wasn't easy. Rehearsal space in Los Angeles is very costly. So, Jeff, John, Nick, and Justin sang wherever they could—in fast food restaurants, parks, even at the zoo! They started to have some minor success—even opening for James Brown at one point. But they weren't gaining the attention of the people in the recording industry. And if you want to be a star, you've got to have a record label backing you.

In 1996, about six months after Nick and

Justin joined the group, John Lipman called it quits. He'd decided that his future was in acting, not singing. While the other three group members respected his desire to follow his heart, John's move had left the guys in a jam. They had a big gig coming up at the Los Angeles House of Blues. For a while, they thought they would have to give up the job while they searched for a new group member. Then, suddenly, Nick got a brilliant idea. He picked up the phone and called his younger brother Drew.

Drew was busy working as an emergency medical technician in Brooklyn, New York. He was happy there, but Nick knew that Drew's true love was music. He also knew that his brother's amazing baritone voice was just the sound the group needed.

Drew didn't need much convincing.

"I got the call, quit my job, closed my bank account, packed my car, and picked up Nick at Newark airport," Drew remembers. "Nick didn't want me to do the drive alone, and the cross-country trip gave me the time and opportunity to learn the songs."

Two days after Drew joined the band, he found himself onstage at the House of Blues.

The performance was a huge success. It was obvious that the addition of Drew to the group had given them the exact sound they'd been looking for all along. But the guys also knew that a record label executive wasn't likely to just stumble into one of their gigs and offer them a deal.

Jeff, Justin, Nick, and Drew had gotten tired of waiting for their big break. It was time for them to go out and make things happen!

3

Take Me Out to the Ball Game

Nick, Justin, Jeff, and Drew had their sound together, but they weren't quite ready for the big time yet. They still needed a good name that was easy for people to remember and represented the feel of their music. After coming up with a few choices that just didn't seem to fit, they finally chose 98 Degrees. As Nick explains, "[We chose the name 98 Degrees because] it kind of describes the atmosphere we want our music to create."

"A lot of the songs we sing are love songs," Drew adds, "and they have to do with the heart and body temperature, which is 98 degrees."

Now that the band had a new name, they

were ready to take on the biggest audience they could find. But rather than continue playing the dance clubs in L.A., the guys went straight for the largest arena they could think of—Dodger Stadium.

"We called Dodger Stadium [to find out about singing the national anthem at a baseball game] and they said they had booked the whole season up," Nick recalls. "But we went down to the corporate offices and started singing in the lobby, and people started coming out from the halls. We got a call a couple of days later. We had a choice of three games!"

98 Degrees chose to sing at a game in which the L.A. Dodgers played the Cincinnati Reds. (No surprise there, huh?)

"We were extremely nervous," Jeff says, remembering the day the guys sang the "Star Spangled Banner" at Dodger Stadium. "I don't think I've ever been that nervous. I'm kind of a shy person, but as things went on, I sort of came out of my shell."

Surprisingly, even singing for 50,000 Dodgers fans wasn't enough to get 98 Degrees a recording deal. (Was it possible that not a single recording exec was present at the game that day?) Still, the guys refused to give up. They plugged on, singing and winning at talent contests in L.A., all the while working jobs like landscaping, delivering Chinese food, and doing security at trendy L.A. nightclubs.

Then, finally, in late 1996, the guys made a move that would change their lives forever. It all started with a couple of tickets to a Boyz II Men concert. . . .

Boyz II Men concert . . .

Mighty Motown

In 1996, Motown recording artists Boyz II
Men were the hottest group in R&B. Nick,
Drew, Jeff, and Justin were (and remain)
huge fans of the group. So when the guys
heard that Boyz II Men would be in L.A.,
they just had to go to the show.

98 Degrees' great desire to go to the
concert was two-fold. First, they wanted to
hear some phenomenal music! But they also
figured that if they could get backstage and
do some singing, maybe someone in Boyz II
Men would take a liking to the 98 Degrees
sound, and help the guys get a meeting with
an agent or a record label exec.

After the show, the guys bravely made
their attempt to get backstage. But since

they did not have backstage passes, they were met with a very cold reception.

"We kept singing for the security guard," Jeff says. "And the guy who was in charge of promotion for the concert was like, 'Give it up. You're not getting backstage. Period.'"

The guys never did get their wish to meet and sing for Boyz II Men. But they did manage to get backstage. They told their story to a deejay from a local radio station, and he asked the guys to perform live on the air.

98 Degrees' performance on the radio caught the attention of Paris D'Jon, who co-managed Montell Jordan and other R&B artists. Paris contacted the guys and said he was interested in representing them. Nick, Drew, Justin, and Jeff were impressed with the roster of R&B performers Paris represented, and soon a partnership was formed. 98 Degrees were on their way!

Not long after that very first meeting with Paris, the guys headed out on the road as the opening act for Montell Jordan. In city after city they received rave reviews for their shows, a rare occurrence for an opening act.

While 98 Degrees were on the road singing and dancing their hearts out, Paris was busy shopping their demo tape around to major record labels. The interest from the recording industry was almost immediate. Three major labels were ready to sign 98 Degrees on the basis of the tape and a single audition. Now, 98 Degrees most certainly had a recording contract. The question was, which label would they choose?

For Jeff, Justin, Drew, and Nick the decision was swift and unanimous—they wanted to record for Motown Records.

"A lot of Motown artists have been a great influence on us," Justin says. "So for us to be able to represent Motown and all that it's stood for over the years is a great honor."

"Motown is an historical legacy," Jeff adds, "and we are proud to be part of it."

Making the decision to join Motown was obviously a no-brainer for 98 Degrees. And it was a smart move. In the forty years since Motown Records was formed, the label has probably had more of an influence on music than any single record company in the history of modern music.

The Motown story began in Detroit,

Michigan, in 1958, when Berry Gordy, Jr. wrote a song called "Lonely Teardrops" for a singer named Jackie Wilson. The song became a million seller, and Berry Gordy went on to write another hit for a singer named Marv Johnson.

Berry Gordy soon came to the realization that he could make a whole lot more money if he created his own label. He borrowed $800 and created Motown Records. Berry came up with his company's name by combining the words *Motor Town*. That's the nickname for Detroit, the city Berry operated Motown from.

Over the years, Motown became home to some of the most famous African-American artists of all time, and introduced rhythm and blues to white audiences. Diana Ross and the Supremes, the Temptations, the Four Tops, Gladys Knight and the Pips, and the Jackson Five were all R&B vocal groups who were discovered by Berry Gordy. Stevie Wonder, another of Berry Gordy's protégés, was a one-man R&B dynamo, taking the world by storm in 1963, when he was only 13 years old. Berry Gordy called Motown's music "The Sound of Young America," but everybody else called it "The Motown Sound."

By the mid-1970s, Berry Gordy's little $800 investment had become the largest black-owned corporation in America. And although over the years the company's headquarters moved to New York City and many of those early Motown acts left the label, Motown was always able to find new exciting talent to take their place. The Commodores, Debarge, and Lionel Richie were all part of the new Motown sound of the '70s and '80s. In the 1990s, Boyz II Men, Queen Latifah, and of course, 98 Degrees carry on the Motown torch.

To some people, the fact that Motown signed on 98 Degrees may seem a bit odd. After all, the guys *are* the only all-white group in the Motown stable. But Nick's feeling is that the Motown execs weren't looking at 98 Degrees' race, they were listening to their music.

"I don't think [race] really matters. I think that our talent comes through, and the label signs the talent, not your skin color. I think Motown recognized that, and that's why they signed us," he explains.

Which is not to say that everything was completely cozy and comfortable right from the beginning.

"I think initially it was kind of a strange situation for us and for the label because it was a new thing," Nick admits. "But we learned a great deal through the course of being together in a relationship. For us it is a great honor because R&B music is the music we grew up on and it's the type of music we like to sing. So to be on Motown Records is the ultimate compliment and the ultimate support for our kind of music."

A Wonder-Ful Beginning!

Nick wasn't kidding when he said Motown would support 98 Degrees' music. For both their first album, *98 Degrees*, and their follow-up hit CD *98 Degrees and Rising*, the label provided the guys with several producers, all of whom acted as both teammates and mentors to Nick, Drew, Jeff, and Justin. The guys got the chance to work with a diverse group of top-level producers that included the Trackmasters (who had previously produced hits for Will Smith and LL Cool J), the Fugees' Pras Michel, Keith Thomas (producer for Brian Mc-Knight and Vanessa Williams), and Anders Bagge (who has produced songs for Robyn).

According to Bruce Carbone, Motown's senior A&R Vice President, hiring the top producers was Motown's way of priming 98 Degrees for a long, successful career.

"It makes them grow more quickly as artists," he explains. "And it always helps to have a little extra incentive to kick off a song. But most of all it shows that this new group can stand up with the best of them and hold their own."

There was also another motive for using several producers who are each known for a specific kind of sound. Motown was hoping that having so many unique-sounding songs would guarantee world-wide success for 98 Degrees.

"We are looking to make records that work globally," Bruce Carbone says.

For their part, 98 Degrees was looking to make their first CD a showcase that would demonstrate their versatile musical style. In the end, both Motown and the group got what they wanted.

"We are pleased that our individual personalities are reflected in the songs on the album," Drew told a crowd of reporters when 98 Degrees was first released. "It will help listeners get familiar with each of our voices and really understand each of the members and how they contribute to 98 Degrees."

Obviously, taking on 98 Degrees was a gamble for Motown Records. But it was a gamble that paid off. Motown released the group's first single, "Invisible Man" on June 24, 1997. The album 98 Degrees was released a month later on July 29, 1997. The single climbed slowly up the charts, finally reaching its peak at number twelve. "Invisible Man" stayed on the Billboard charts for twelve weeks, earning the boys their first gold record.

Motown quickly packed the boys off for a tour of Europe and Asia, where they soon became one of the hottest acts around.

Still, in their home country, 98 Degrees had not hit the big time—at least not with the kind of popularity other bands like the Backstreet Boys were seeing.

"Our main problem was we had that big record ("Invisible Man") and nobody [in the U.S.] knew who the guys were," Paris

D'Jon explains. "Our faces just weren't out there."

So Motown jumped in, making a big effort to get the guys more radio and video play back home. They arranged for 98 Degrees to record "Was It Something I Didn't Say" for the soundtrack to the short-lived TV show, *Fame, L.A.* The song was written by award-winning song writer Diane Warren.

Motown wanted the song, and the video that went along with it, released as soon as possible. So the company did something rarely seen in the music business. Rather than wait to put "Was It Something I Didn't Say" on 98 Degrees' second album, they pulled the group's first CD off the shelves. The company then quickly added "Was It Something I Didn't Say" to *98 Degrees*. The CD was re-issued on March 10, 1998, with the new song in place. (FYI: If you happen to have a copy of the original version of *98 Degrees*, hold on to it and keep it in good condition, it should be worth quite a bit to collectors someday!)

Motown then started a big publicity campaign around the re-release of *98 Degrees*. They arranged for the guys to sing the national anthem at a sporting event once again. Only this time the performance was nationally televised to a huge audience because 98 Degrees was singing at game five of the Chicago Bulls/Utah Jazz NBA finals.

The strategy paid off. "Was It Something I Didn't Say" became the guys' second song to reach the *Billboard* Top 20.

And Motown wasn't finished yet. The company still had another major trick up its sleeve. Walt Disney Pictures had approached Motown, requesting a new, fresh group to record "True To Your Heart," the song that would run during the closing titles in its new animated film, *Mulan.* Motown suggested 98 Degrees.

Recording a Disney song in itself would have meant tremendous exposure for Nick, Drew, Jeff, and Justin. After all, a Disney film brings publicity to everyone who is a part of it. And the song would appear on the soundtrack for the film, guaranteeing the guys a large, built-in audience.

But Motown had an idea that would create an even bigger stir. They decided to team 98 Degrees up with one of their big-name internationally established R&B acts.

"They initially suggested the Temptations," Drew says, "But we're already a four-part group, and we wouldn't have been able to have as much harmony among ourselves."

So Motown suggested that the legendary Stevie Wonder share the bill with 98 Degrees. And after hearing a few cuts from the guys' first CD, Stevie agreed to take part in "True To Your Heart."

Nick says he will never forget the first time he heard the final version of "True To Your Heart."

"It was an awesome feeling to hear your voice with Stevie Wonder's, exchanging riffs and singing harmony parts together. It was completely unreal," he recalls.

The experience became even more amazing when 98 Degrees was offered the chance to join Stevie Wonder and sing "True To Your Heart" on *The Tonight Show with Jay Leno*.

"That was the biggest adrenaline rush I've had since I've been doing this," Jeff admits. "I couldn't help but think, 'What am I doing here?'"

Red Hot and Getting Hotter!

It was time to strike while the iron was hot (98 Degrees hot, that is!). So the guys began a marathon recording session—finishing their sophomore effort, *98 Degrees and Rising,* in just two and a half months. They recorded in studios all over the country, including New York, Nashville, and Los Angeles.

Justin, Nick, Drew, and Jeff are quick students. They had learned a lot from the producers who helped them record their first album. Their successes had built their confidence in their own musical abilities. So when it came time to record their second CD, they recorded several songs that they had written by themselves and with others.

They were also far bolder about making production suggestions than they were the first time around.

"We definitely took a more hands-on approach," Jeff recalls.

"We got to do a lot more writing and producing [on *98 Degrees and Rising*]," Justin adds. "We have a lot more variety on there. A lot more up temps, great dance tunes."

"And there's some a capella," Drew continues, particularly referring to the group's remake of Michael Jackson's "She's Out Of My Life." "That's where we started at. It's a sound we're very comfortable with. That's a staple to prove to people you really can sing."

But even with upbeat tunes and a capella harmonies, the 98 Degrees guys knew that their fans would be clamoring for some beautiful ballads. And they did not disappoint. Ballads like "Because Of You," "Still," and "I Do (Cherish You)" are the kinds of songs that would warm the heart of any romantic!

"No matter what, ballads are definitely

our strong point," Justin explains. "We are all suckers for love songs."

While 98 Degrees was in the studio, Motown was working hard to get the fans psyched for the anticipated October release of the new CD. Throughout the summer, a thirty-five-foot bus wrapped in a giant *98 Degrees and Rising* album cover was parked outside concerts by the Backstreet Boys, the Spice Girls, and Janet Jackson. Motown figured 98 Degrees would attract the same audience as those already established acts. The bus was a real attention getter—until someone's Ford pick-up plowed into its side.

"If this had been last year [1997], we would have been in big trouble," Paris D'Jon told *Billboard* magazine. "We were living in that bus!"

98 Degrees spent part of the summer performing at malls and cheerleading camps around the country in a tour sponsored by *Seventeen* magazine. Meeting up with high school girls guaranteed 98 Degrees would have plenty of word of mouth publicity when the cheerleaders got back to school. The guys must have put on some pretty hot shows, because it's rumored that Drew had

to use some of his old EMT resuscitation skills when one of their fans passed out during a performance at a cheerleading camp.

"Because Of You" was released on September 15, 1998. The single shot its way up the *Billboard* Hot 100 like a rocket, finally finding its way to the number three spot!

98 Degrees was thrilled that they were finally getting the notoriety in their own country they had always desired. But they didn't forget how faithful their Asian fans had been during the past year. So they dashed off for a quick "thank you" tour of the region—introducing the new single, and celebrating the international release of *Mulan*.

This time around, the guys felt very at home in the countries they toured. They had a blast, making sure that they took time to revisit some of their favorite clubs, and eat at a few of the most memorable restaurants. (This time around they actually had enough cash to order some of the more expensive items on the menu!)

"My favorite [country on the tour] was Singapore because it was really clean and

you knew no one was gonna get out of line,"
Drew told an AOL chat audience.

"Thailand had the best food," Jeff added.
"I loved the spicy chicken."

Justin told the fans in the chat room that
he loved all the cities the guys visited but,
"Indonesia was my favorite because the fans
there were the craziest."

Still, it's Nick who probably could have a
great career in diplomacy. He refused to
choose a favorite country, saying simply, "In
all honesty it's hard to pick—each country
had so many different things to offer."

The success of "Because Of You" made
fans all over the world very hungry for *98
Degrees and Rising* to hit the stores. On
October 27, their waiting was rewarded
with the album's release.

The CD earned rave reviews, with *Entertainment Weekly* calling 98 Degrees "the
most elegant of the boy bands." (A nice
compliment for sure, but isn't everybody
sick of that term "boy bands" by now?)

To make sure that this time around everyone knew who 98 Degrees was, Motown
arranged for the boys to make the rounds of
all the major talk shows. They appeared on

Ricki Lake, Live with Regis and Kathie Lee, The View, The Howie Mandel Show, and *Soul Train.* They were also the featured performers on MTV's *Total Request Live* and *Loveline.*

Holiday parade watchers had a chance to catch 98 Degrees fever as well. Drew, Nick, Justin, and Jeff were the featured performers on the Planters Peanuts float in the Macy's Thanksgiving Day Parade. Less than a month later, they were seen in the UPN Hollywood Christmas parade.

But just hearing 98 Degrees sing a song or two on a TV show or onboard a passing parade float was not enough to satisfy the fans. So the guys took to the road on a limited engagement winter tour from December 1998 through January 1999. Drew, Nick, Justin, and Jeff played arenas and theaters in major cities throughout the U.S., including stops in Washington, D.C., Philadelphia, Baltimore, Cleveland, and Walt Disney World in Florida. They sang the national anthem on *Monday Night Football,* and put in an appearance at New York City's famed Jingle Ball, an annual holiday charity concert at Madison Square Garden. At the

Jingle Ball the guys shared the stage with other red hot groups like 'N Sync and Barenaked Ladies.

But the winter tour was limited in scope, and 98 Degrees knew that some fans were disappointed that the guys didn't come to their hometowns. So 98 Degrees quickly announced a major spring tour with dates that would take the boys all over the U.S. and Canada, beginning on March 16, 1999. The minute the dates were announced on the official 98 Degrees Web site, they set off a phone flurry, with fans calling their local arenas, trying to find out when they could purchase tickets.

Teen magazines were suddenly making the most of 98 Degrees' new-found success. Almost all the mags featured posters and pin-ups of the guys in their year-end issues. *Pop Stars* magazine devoted a whole issue to the boys, and *Bop* magazine featured "Invisible Man" on their *Bop Boys* compilation CD and video.

On December 3, 1998, "Because Of You" went platinum, meaning one million copies of the single had been sold. The momentum of the single pushed the *98 Degrees and*

Rising album to gold status (five hundred thousand copies sold).

Later that same month, Motown celebrated the fact that 98 *Degrees and Rising* had achieved gold album status by throwing a huge party at the Motown Cafe in midtown Manhattan. Naturally, Jeff, Justin, Drew, and Nick were the guests of honor.

Let's face it, if you got an invitation to a party and you knew the 98 Degrees guys were going to be there, you'd go, right? Well, that's exactly how all the invited guests felt. On the night of the party, the upper level of the Motown Cafe was filled with record execs and members of the press. Photographers clicked photos of 98 Degrees posing with their gold album. The group members mingled like pros, chatting with everyone and being especially careful to sincerely thank all of the teen magazine editors who had been so helpful in bringing the group to their readers' attention during the past year.

The upstairs shindig was definitely a fun time, but the truth is the real party was going on *outside* the restaurant. That's where literally hundreds of fans were lined up, hoping to get a glimpse of their favorite 98 Degrees hunks. The fans brought portable CD players and blasted *98 Degrees and Rising* through the city streets, joining in with the music until the line turned into a giant sing-along. The best moment of all for the fans came when the guys stepped outside. They signed autographs and serenaded everyone with an a capella rendition of "Because Of You."

It just goes to show that even though the press and record execs were in their corner, the guys knew who had really turned *98 Degrees and Rising* into gold. *The fans!* They were the ones who had saved their allowance and baby-sitting money to buy the CD in the first place.

By going out to meet and greet the fans, Justin, Drew, Jeff, and Nick proved to the world that they really were the nice guys they claimed to be. Even the press vouches for their sincerity.

"Not only are these guys really talented, but they are the nicest group of guys you'd ever want to meet," Matt Rossman, managing editor of *Teen Beat* magazine, assures their fans.

In late December 1998, Polygram records (the parent company of Motown Records) merged with Universal Records. As part of the Motown family, 98 Degrees had now joined the roster of Universal recording artists. But none of that changed 98 Degrees' plans. In fact, being part of a new larger company allowed the Motown folks to plan an even bigger publicity blitz for the radio-only release of the third single from *98 Degrees and Rising*, "The Hardest Thing," which was due out on February 23, 1999.

By 1999, the stakes had become a lot higher. It was clear to everyone who knew them that 98 Degrees had moved into a whole new league. 98 Degrees *were* the Motown sound of the millennium! And there was no stopping the heat!

The 411 on the Feverish Four

Which one of the 98 Degrees guys has been linked to Jennifer Love Hewitt and Mariah Carey in the press? Who's the biggest flirt in 98 Degrees? Which guy almost went into medicine as a career? Which of the group members do the guys in 98 Degrees consider their "father figure"?

If you've been searching for the answers to these burning questions, you can stop looking. You've come to the right place. We've got all your answers right here.

Jeff: The Leader of the Pack

Jeffrey Brandon Timmons
Birthday: April 30, 1973

Weight: **160 pounds**
Height: **5'8"**
Hair: **Brown**
Eyes: **Blue**
Lucky Number: **Seven**
Sings: **Second lead and falsetto**
Parents: **Jim and Trish**
Siblings: **Older brother Mike, younger
    sister Kristina**

An All American Boy

Massillon, Ohio, is not exactly a big town. In
fact, if you ask people where Jeffrey Brandon Timmons was born, they'll probably say
nearby Canton, Ohio, because not too many
people are familiar with Massillon.

But Massillon is Jeffrey's hometown. It's
where he and his siblings grew up. (Just
in case you thought Jeff's striking good
looks were some sort of genetic fluke, consider this: brother Mike is an actor and a
model, and sister Kristina is a model and a
nurse.)

Jeff's growing up was sitcom perfect—
you know, mom, dad, sibs, dogs, the whole
bit! He played football in high school and

was in the choir. Singing in choir was fun,
but Jeff says it didn't particularly make him
want to go into music full time.

"I never even dreamed of being a singer,
EVER!" he insists. "I wanted to be a pro
football player. That was my goal in life—
until a few years ago."

Jeff was always a really popular guy. Way
back in his first year of high school he was
voted "outstanding freshman boy." Over
the years he won many awards in high
school, including the "rising star" award
(how prophetic is that?!) Here's a surprise,
though: that award wasn't for Jeff's singing,
it was for acting in the school play!

But this guy who was voted "prettiest
eyes" in his senior class yearbook (a title no
one who has ever gazed into those baby
blues could ever argue with!) was not without his troubles growing up. His first date
was a disaster! His mom set him up with the
daughter of a friend, and according to Jeff,
"she didn't dig me at all." (Hard to believe,
isn't it?) And he still tears up when he thinks
about the girl who dumped him in high
school without warning. She just liked
someone else better. (Even *more* difficult to

believe!) The breakup was painful, and it was made worse because Jeff saw this girl and her new boyfriend every day!

Jeff also cringes when he recalls failing his very first driving test. He says he "just panicked." Luckily, he passed the test the second time around. Good thing. Imagine how geeky it would have been to be a senior without a license. No car dates!

Jeff is really grateful to his mom, Trish, and his dad, Jim, for giving him such a stable family life. In fact, to this day, his most prized possessions are not jewels or cars, but the pictures of his family that he carries with him wherever he goes.

Jeff the Shrink

Most people think of high school football players as "jocks" who care more about touchdowns and end zones than they do about people and their feelings. But Jeff wasn't at all like that. He has always been concerned with people's emotions, and what makes them tick. That's why he decided to be a psychology major at Kent State

University. But Jeff is kind of glad he never went into psychology as a profession. "Was I good at it?" he says. "Nah. Not really."

What Jeff *was* good at, though, was singing. In fact, he has such a great musical ear that he can hear a single wrong note—and tell you who sang it! When Jeff started singing with a few guys in college, he came to an intense realization. Music was his life! This was what he really wanted to do.

Taurus Traits

As just about everyone knows by now, Jeff and a few friends quit school that year and made their way to Los Angeles in the hopes of becoming singing sensations. One by one Jeff's friends gave up on their dreams and moved away.

But not Jeff. He stuck with it, keeping food on the table and a roof over his head by delivering food and working as a security guard. His good looks also got him a few commercial gigs, including one for the U.S. Navy. But none of those jobs were steady or well-paying. Which meant that super carnivore Jeff had to go without his favorite food—steak! Still Jeff never gave up. And his perseverance paid off—in the form of 98 Degrees. (Sometimes he eats three steaks a day now, he says.)

That stick-with-it attitude is something that comes with Jeff's Taurus pedigree. People born under the Taurus sun sign are known for their ability to overcome seemingly overwhelming odds. And as anyone who has ever tried to make it in the music business can tell you, the odds of making it big are not good. Taurians don't always play by the rules however. And Jeff thinks that's part of why 98 Degrees has been so successful.

"A lot of people who are trying to make it, follow the rules," he says. "We didn't even know there *were* rules!"

Taurians pride themselves on being able to exert control over any situation, and they often wind up leaders, whether they plan it that way or not. When it comes to 98 Degrees, Jeff is definitely the leader. After all, it was Jeff who started the whole ball rolling. And it was Jeff who kept plugging away, insisting that if the guys could just get themselves heard, they would be a success.

"I never really rest," Jeff admits.

"Jeff is one of the most loyal, hardworking people you'll ever meet," Drew says.

Are You the Girl for Jeff?

Jeff knows that all work and no play makes for one dull pop star! So he keeps his spontaneous side busy, too. How spontaneous? Well, one time he spotted a beautiful girl in a mall and just started serenading her.

"I felt that if I passed up that opportunity, I never would have seen her again," he explains.

The girl in question was definitely flattered, and she and Jeff actually dated for a while. But just because Jeff was uninhibited enough to sing a capella in a mall one day doesn't mean that you should try spontaneous *physical* contact with him should you two meet up.

"One time at an amusement park this girl came out of nowhere and kissed me. She was a stranger, so I thought it was a little odd," he recalls. "The girl was cute, and she definitely caught my attention, but it was a little forward for me."

So what *does* attract Jeff? Romance! He's a real roses and candy kind of guy. And he kind of likes it when his girlfriend is creative. He has never forgotten the girl who planned a very special birthday celebration for him.

"On my birthday she sprinkled rose petals all the way up the walkway to the door of her apartment," he recalled to *Teen Celebrity* magazine. "She had cooked up a great dinner, and we ate by candlelight, and she got me one of those big heart-shaped cookies that said, 'Happy Birthday, I Love You.' I'll never forget that night as long as I live."

Although Jeff has been linked in the press to famous beauties like Jennifer Love Hewitt (he swears they have never been more than friends), and Mariah Carey (after reading in a tabloid about how she walked over to his table to ask him out, he said, "Boy I wish I'd actually been there!") he says looks don't really matter that much to him. He's more into a nice smile, and pretty eyes. He also likes a girl who's good with a pool cue!

"I like a girl who can hang out and be one of the guys," he says. "You can play pool with her, and she's your best friend.

"I really value a girl's humor and independence," he adds.

Any girl who does capture Jeff's heart is going to need that independence. After all, 98 Degrees is on tour a lot of the year. Jeff's girl will have to be secure enough to know that he cares about her even though he can't always be there. And that's not as easy as it sounds. Jeff is still smarting over a relationship that went sour just after 98 Degrees started their world tour in 1998.

"It's hard to find a girl who will be there to support you even though she's not going to see you for months on end," Jeff explains. "It's harder than this job, harder than any job I've ever had, keeping a relationship going."

Right now, Jeff is single, and always on the lookout. Any takers?

Drew: The Baby of the Band

Andrew John Lachey
Birthday: August 8, 1976

Weight: **148 pounds**
Height: **5'6"**
Hair: **Brown**
Eyes: **Hazel**
Lucky Number: **Six**
Sings: **Baritone**
Parents: **Cate Fopma-Leimbach and John Lachey**
Siblings: **Older brother Nick, younger sisters Josie and Kaitlin, and younger brothers Isaac and Zac**

Hats off to Drew!

Of all the members in 98 Degrees, Drew's the easiest to spot. He's the one with the baseball cap on. But don't be fooled by his big brother Nick's claim that Drew wears baseball hats "to hide his receding hairline." Drew's got a full head of silky brown hair. He just wears baseball caps because he doesn't like to fuss in the mornings.

"I love baseball caps, and the truth is, I'm too lazy to comb my hair," he admits.

Right now, Drew has thirty-five baseball caps in his collection. "I usually buy them to coordinate with what I have on," he explains. "The most special is my Kansas City Chiefs pro model cap."

(FYI: If you're thinking of sending Drew a baseball cap for his birthday or Christmas, he's a size 7.)

Wearing a baseball cap helps Drew stand out in a crowd—or in a group. And that's important to Drew because he's always followed in the footsteps of his talented brother, Nick, who's three years older than Drew.

School Days

Nick and Drew are both really talented guys. They could sing practically as soon as they could talk. But Nick was three years older, and could do things sooner. Growing up, it always seemed as though Drew was copying his big brother.

Still the brothers were very close. Even though Drew and Nick have several siblings and half siblings, Drew was eight years older than his next sibling, Josie. So it was usually Nick and Drew who hung out together.

In Cincinnati, where Drew and Nick grew up, there are many public high schools. Some you go to simply because you live in the neighborhood. Others are specialty schools. You have to have a talent to get into those.

When it came time for high school, Nick chose one of the city's special schools, the School for Creative and Performing Arts. Drew, who was equally talented, entered the school three years after Nick did.

High school was incredibly important to Drew. He always made sure he sat in a spot where he could see the teacher. This helped him concentrate on what he was trying to learn. (He swears it really works—give it a try some time!) And while other kids were dropping out of school, Drew made sure he stayed put.

"High school is just a given," he explains. "You have to get your diploma or your GED because otherwise you'll be flipping burgers for the rest of your life. I don't even know if they let you flip burgers these days without a high school diploma."

But having two brothers with similar talents in the same school set the scene for some intense sibling rivalry. Nick and Drew found themselves sometimes competing for center stage at the same school. They also found themselves competing for the same girls.

One of Drew's saddest high school memories is about a girl he had a major crush on during his freshman year. The girl had a crush, too. But she liked Nick. And before long Drew's big bro snatched the girl right out from under Drew's nose. It caused a lot of hostility between the Lachey sibs, but eventually Nick and the girl broke up, and Drew and Nick managed to patch up their differences.

Today, Nick says that "we got over all that sibling rivalry stuff a long time ago. We are pretty much best friends. Some guys don't live near their brothers, and they only get to see them a few times a year. I'm really glad that Drew's in the group."

But patching up sibling rivalry isn't always easy. In fact, the brothers had to put the whole country between them to realize that they really wanted to be together.

Drew Takes a Bite Out of the Big Apple

Drew had big plans when he graduated from high school. He wanted to move to

New York City. And he wanted to help people.

Drew is a very determined person. When he makes his mind up to do something, he does it. In this case, he moved to Brooklyn, New York, and took courses in emergency medicine.

"You need some sort of skilled training or higher learning other than high school so that you can provide for yourself or your family down the road," he explains of his decision to go on for more education. "Otherwise, you're going to be stuck in a rut and you'll never get out. You'll spend all of your time working so hard just to make ends meet, that you'll never advance yourself."

Working as an emergency medical technician made Drew really happy. Let's face it, there's no bigger rush than saving another human being's life. (It was probably a rush for some of his patients too. Hey, if someone had to give you mouth to mouth resuscitation, wouldn't you like it to be Drew?!)

But something was missing. Drew wasn't singing all that much anymore. Music was in Drew's soul. He needed to sing, dance, and perform almost as much as he needed food and water. And so, when his big brother Nick made that fateful phone call, asking him to join 98 Degrees, Drew just couldn't say no. That was lucky for all those 98 Degrees fans out there. After all, as Nick has often said, Drew was "the piece that finished the 98 Degrees puzzle."

Learnin' About Leos

Drew's birthday places him smack dab in the middle of the sun sign Leo. And Drew is one true Leo!

Leos are known to be highly dramatic people. They love center stage. That's surely true in Drew's case. Anyone who has ever seen Drew perform can tell you that when Drew takes over a solo, his eyes light up like a Christmas tree. For Drew, the stage is home.

Leos are also well known for their organizational skills. "Be prepared" may be the boy scout motto, but it could be a Leo's motto as well.

Jeff has said that he thinks of Drew as "the fatherly figure of the group. He's so organized. I look up to him that way."

Even big brother Nick has to concede that without Drew's organizational skills, 98 Degrees might not sound as together as they do.

"Drew represents the organization of 98 Degrees," Nick boasts about his little bro. "He's always the one who makes sure we're all on the same page of music."

But before you get to thinking that Leos are all work and no play, consider this: Leos are extremely impulsive, colorful people. Maybe that explains why Justin calls Drew "absolutely the most fun in the group. He's such a smart aleck!"

Drew does have a good sense of humor. At five foot six inches tall, he could be paranoid about being the shortest member of 98 Degrees—especially since the others have bestowed the nickname Sprout upon him. But Drew just laughs the whole height thing off. In fact, he recently joked with a reporter that if the Spice Girls were looking for a replacement for Ginger Spice, he was volunteering to be Shorty Spice!

Drew's silly sense of humor also lends itself well to playing practical jokes. He's been known to staple Nick, Jeff, and Justin's clothing to the floor, and to pour green, slimy goo on them when they least expect it.

So watch out for Drew. You never know what he's going to do next!

Are You the Girl for Drew?

These days, Drew is definitely single—and looking! That's music to the ears of his thousands of female fans. But before you slip Drew that piece of paper with your phone number on it, there's a few things you should know.

First and foremost, Drew can't stand being around people who are self-centered or snobby. Drew cares more about others than he does about himself. And that's something he looks for in a girlfriend as well.

Drew also likes a girl who knows her own mind, and isn't shy about standing up for what she believes.

"I like a girl who has opinions about things," he says. "I don't like a girl who will go along with something just because that's what everyone else is doing."

Drew says a girl doesn't have to be model-perfect to catch his eye. She just has to be "a girl who loves life and has a great sense of humor." (A girl would *have* to have a sense of humor if her boyfriend might get her with green goo at a moment's notice!)

If you're getting ready for a big date with Drew, here's a helpful hint. Brush your teeth and get yourself a nice manicure. Drew feels that bad breath and dirty nails are total turn-offs!

And be sure to get yourself a good pair of sneakers and a new bathing suit. Drew is very athletic, and he says his dream girl would be too. Drew loves water sports, especially waterskiing. In the wintertime, put on your parka and get set for some high-speed snowboarding!

Drew's dream vacation spot is a little cabin in the mountains, far from cars and noise. It's the perfect spot for two people to get to know each other and really talk. But if you ever are lucky enough to have Drew all to yourself, be sure to always call him Drew and never Andy! He hates that name!

Another topic to stay away from is boy bands. Where 98 Degrees is concerned, that's a label Drew can't stand.

"We formed on our own. We have fans

from four to fifty-four, and we perform and sing live at our shows. This boy band labeling doesn't sit well with us at all," he exclaims.

Instead, you might want to talk about Drew's favorite sports team, the Kansas City Chiefs. Or bring along a copy of his favorite video, Mel Gibson's *Braveheart*. He'll watch it over and over again.

The girl that finally captures Drew's heart will surely be in for a lot of fun and games. Drew never feels like he's too old for a good old-fashioned snowball battle or a pillow fight.

"The girl for me must like having a good time," Drew insists. "I love fun."

Which might explain Drew's motto in life: "Man doesn't cease to play because he grows old. He grows old because he ceases to play!"

Party on, Drew!

Justin: The Big Flirt!

Justin Paul Jeffre
Birthday: February 25, 1973
Height: 5'10"

Weight: **150 pounds**
Hair: **Brown**
Eyes: **Blue**
Lucky Number: **Seven**
Sings: **Bass**
Parents: **Sue and Dan Jeffre**
Siblings: **Older sister Ann, older brother
   Dan, older brother Jeff, younger sister
   Alexandrea**

Living a Superstar's Life!

When 98 Degrees first made it big, Justin
bought himself something he had always
wanted—a pair of $300 sunglasses! Most
guys would have gone for the big car, the
house with a swimming pool, or the jet. But
Justin just wanted those glasses.

People who know Justin wouldn't be surprised by that. They know that Justin isn't
into music for the bucks. He's doing it
because ever since he was three years old,
he's been singing and dancing his way into
people's hearts. When he was little, he
would perform holiday songs for his family
every Christmas.

"I have all that on tape," he admits. (Hey

Justin, why not release the tapes on CD?! We'd love to hear them!)

Like Nick and Drew, Big J attended Cincinnati's School for Creative and Performing Arts. He was accepted on the merits of his wonderfully deep booming voice, which he's had since he was a teenager. (Even as a kid Justin's voice was so low he was often mistaken for his dad on the phone!) While he was in school, Justin sang in lots of groups, including an oldies cover band, and a barbershop quartet. He even used to spend time in the boys' bathroom, singing pop tunes in the mirror with Nick! As far as Justin was concerned, it didn't matter what kind of music he was singing, as long as it was good music.

And although people at the school always found Justin to be a great talent, they say he was remarkably low key about superstardom. He was one of those guys who was into art for art's sake.

But today, even super-cool Justin has to admit that being a superstar does have its advantages. But not in the way you might think. Justin isn't into using his stardom to pick up girls or get good tables at fancy night spots. He wants to use his mega-popularity to influence people to do good deeds.

"I want [98 Degrees] to be big enough where we can really have an impact on certain things," he explains.

In keeping with that truly beautiful senti-ment, Justin says he is more proud of the 98 Degrees Foundation than he is of anything else the group has accomplished.

The 98 Degrees Foundation is a charity group organized by the boys to help those less fortunate—particularly children. In the beginning, the four guys went around to hospitals and sang for sick kids. But as their popularity has increased, the foundation has been able to organize more large-scale pro-grams, like a coat drive for underprivileged and homeless kids. Justin is also proud that the 98 Degrees fan club newsletter includes information about how fans can get involved in their communities.

"I always want to make a difference. Everyone can make a difference," Justin declares to his fans.

It's Not All Glory!

Although Justin is thrilled with all the great things celebrity has allowed him to do, he knows that there is a downside to being a star.

"Once in a while you miss normal things," he admits, "like going out with your friends on the weekend. But it is worth it."

There are also the screaming fans. When 98 Degrees first landed in Manila in 1997, they were followed everywhere they went by over-enthusiastic fans. Justin admits that while it was flattering to have so many women screaming his name, it was also a bit intimidating. Nothing like that had ever happened to him before. Suddenly the guys were traveling with bodyguards wherever they went!

So, in some ways it was a relief to return to the states where the boys were still comparatively "Invisible Men." But, by the time *98 Degrees and Rising* was released, the guys were well known in their homeland, too. Their freedom of movement was really limited. They couldn't even go to a record store without being recognized. Which, while extremely cool, can be a little scary.

There's also the issue of rumors. Rumors about the group are everywhere—and Justin wants everyone to know that "not everything you read on the internet is true." But he tries not to let the rumors of in-fighting or celebrity dating get to him. "We try to ignore all the rumors. The truth is scary enough," he jokes, adding seriously, "If you start listening to the rumors, you can't be true to yourself."

The Perplexing Pisces!

Of all the signs of the zodiac, Pisces is the sign that represents dreams and secrets. It is the sign of things that are hidden.

Justin is known as the cool, calm, collected member of 98 Degrees. But like all Pisces, his outward demeanor is hiding a big secret—which we are about to reveal!

Justin can be a wild man!

As Jeff says, "[Justin] may seem calm, but he loves to party!"

When Justin is in party mode, watch out!

98°

Jeff

Justin

Nick

Drew

Red-Hot!

He'll usually turn on a James Brown CD and get the dancing started. James Brown, better known as "the hardest working man in show business," is one of Justin's favorite R&B artists.

"I love the funky music of James Brown!" he exclaims. "He's my idol. When we opened for him it was a dream come true!"

Pisces is a water sign, and like water, Pisces people tend to go with the flow. When the others are nervous or upset about something, it is Justin they turn to for advice. Justin is a logical kind of guy, and he gives well thought out suggestions.

"I am very calm and natural," he explains. "I think things over a lot. Before making a decision, I think of the positives and the negatives."

Pisces have a great connection to the past, and Justin is no exception. His decision to be a history major in college was pretty typical for a Pisces. Like most Pisces, Justin has a great need to make sense of the world around him. He thinks history can help him do that.

"[I majored in history] just to have a knowledge of things. I don't think you can really have an understanding of what's going on in the world today unless you know something about history."

Justin isn't just interested in world history, he has a great sense of nostalgia for his own personal history. That's why he, more than anyone, was resistant to the guys' move to New York City in 1997.

Motown records had convinced the guys to move to New York soon after they signed with the label. Publicity-wise, that was a good move because most of the U.S. press operates out of New York City. Motown also has major corporate offices there. But while you can take the guys out of Ohio, you just can't take the Ohio out of the guys. And when the idea came up for 98 Degrees to do their rehearsing in the auditorium of Justin's alma mater—the School for Creative and Performing Arts—Justin was on the next plane out. He still says he'd love to move back to Ohio one day.

Are You the Girl for Justin?

Pisces often display remarkable musical talent (no big shocker there, huh?). And they are extremely creative. They are also big into dream interpretation.

Are you into dreams? Dreams like you dating Justin? Well, if you do meet up with Justin, be gentle. He's had a very rocky love life. In fact, he says he can't even count the number of times he's had his heart broken.

In high school, Justin was one of those guys who worshipped girls from afar. He was so shy, he found it hard to ask anyone out on a date.

But that's all over now. According to Justin, "I used to be shy around girls. But I'm more confident now."

Is he ever! When the guys in 98 Degrees were asked by a reporter who was the biggest flirt in the group, the decision was easy! Drew, Jeff, and Nick all agreed that Justin was the big flirt.

Justin didn't deny it completely. But when the other guys said that he winked at all the girls from the stage, Justin replied, "Not *all* the girls!"

Okay, Justin, only *most* of the girls!

Justin says his kind of girl is funny, honest,

and intelligent. "I like a girl who can be deep and serious, but not all the time. I want a girl who knows how to have fun."

But if you're a smoker, you'd better quit before you get close to Justin. "Girls who smoke turn me off!" he declares.

If you want to know the real way to Justin's heart, it's through his stomach. Give him a bowl of Cincinnati Skyline Chili, and watch him smile.

"You haven't tasted Skyline Chili until you've had it in Cincinnati," he swears.

The girl who grabs Justin's heart had better be sure to have her suitcase packed at all times! Justin loves traveling. When the guys are away gigging, he's the first one to want to leave the hotel and check things out. He says his dream vacation would be a safari through the jungle.

Sounds perfect for a guy with such incredible animal magnetism!

Nick: The Jock

Nicholas Scott Lachey
Birthday: November 9, 1973

Weight: **180 pounds**
Height: **5'10"**
Hair: **Brown**
Eyes: **Blue**
Lucky Number: **Eight**
Sings: **Lead**
Parents: **Cate Fopma-Leimbach and John Lachey**
Siblings: **Younger sisters Josie and Kaitlin, and younger brothers Drew, Isaac, and Zac**

The Good Sport

Okay, so how do you pick Nick out of the 98 Degrees crowd? Just look for the muscles. Hands down, this guy has the best bod in the bunch. He's solid muscle. But don't think those pecs and biceps come easy—he works at it! While he may kid around with fans and tell them he gets those washboard abs from from stuff like goat's milk, in reality, it's Nick who is the first one to find the hotel gym, no matter where the guys are staying!

Ever since he was a little boy, Nick's been

into athletics. His fondest memories take place on the field.

"One of my favorite memories is the time when my dad came to see me play in a baseball game and I hit a home run. It was one of those father-son bonding moments," he recalls.

Nick was a terrific baseball player as well as being a starting player on the football team at Cincinnati's School for Creative and Performing Arts. (Nick was also in the choir at the school.) Sports taught Nick a great lesson. He developed into a true team player who could always be depended on—no matter how tough the going got. It's a skill he's carried into 98 Degrees. Even though Nick sings lead, he thinks of the group as a team. Everyone on the team has to pull their own weight or the guys can't win. And as everyone knows, 98 Degrees are total winners!

These days, Nick has very little time for team sports. But he makes do by watching his favorite Cincinnati teams whenever he can. When he was recently asked by a reporter what made him smile, he immediately replied, "When my favorite team wins a big game, it makes me smile." Then he added, "A great song makes me smile. Beautiful girls make me smile." But the true Nick shined through with that immediate response.

Most colleges don't have baseball or football listed as a major in their catalogs. So, when Nick went to Ohio's Miami University, he chose the next best thing, sports medicine. Nick liked the sports medicine curriculum, and the idea of working with athletes seemed like a great idea at the time. But Nick missed the music he'd experienced in high school. For the first time, Nick realized how much music really meant to him. So as soon as he had the opportunity, he packed his bags, left college, and moved to Los Angeles in the hopes of pursuing a musical career.

And by now, we all know how that turned out!

Brotherly Love!

No doubt about it, without Nick, there'd be no 98 Degrees. And not just because he has such a gorgeous, smooth, sexy voice.

There'd be no 98 Degrees because if Nick
had not suggested that his brother Drew join
the band, the guys would never have found
their distinctive sound.

Not too many guys would have suggested
that their little brother horn in on their
careers. After all, asking your little bro to
join a band is not the same as recommending
him for a job at your big corporate office.
Band members travel together, live together, eat together and work together. How'd
you like to be around *your* younger sib that
much?

But Nick really likes Drew. "We're pretty
much best friends," he declares. "It's great
because we are totally there for each other.
It's an 'I got your back' type of thing."

Which is not to say that sibling rivalry
never crops up.

"Drew's had 21 years to know he's inferi-
or," Nick joked to one Malaysian reporter.
"But seriously, we used to fight a lot more
when we were younger, but in the last eight
years we've been more like best buddies."

The brothers even went so far as to go
together to get their first tattoos.

"Drew and I both got an arm band with

the first letter of our last name on it because it was unique to our family," Nick explains. (Nick also has a 98 Degrees logo tattoo.)

Of course, the other guys tease the brothers about their matching body art.

"They really got them so they don't forget their last names," Justin jokes.

But Nick takes the ribbing with a good nature. After all, at this point, all four members of 98 Degrees are together so often, it sometimes seems as though they are *all* brothers.

"We're all like a big family now," Nick says.

Sensitive Scorpio

Nick's early November birthday makes him a Scorpio. Now ordinarily, you might think of Scorpios as the kind of people who can sting like a scorpion. And, on a certain level you would be right. Nick does have a sort of wry sense of humor that sometimes has a little bite to it. But it's all in fun. Like most Scorpios, Nick uses that humor as a kind of armor to protect the sensitive guy hiding inside.

Nick is quite possibly the most sensitive guy in the group. He's the one who worries when fans wait in line in the cold. And he's the one who wants to make sure no one is disappointed—even when circumstances are beyond his control.

"In Indonesia we were there during a time of political unrest. The police wouldn't give us permits to sign autographs because they were afraid of mass crowds gathering and having some sort of rioting situation like they had a couple of weeks prior to us coming," Nick recently told a *Teen Beat* reporter. "It's unfortunate because the fans couldn't know the ins and outs of what was going on. It was frustrating."

Nick so truly cares about his fans that he says he'd play a concert even if just one person showed up (fat chance of that these days, Nick!).

"We'd go on for one person if we had to," he says. "Honestly, we feel that everybody counts, and if we could entertain somebody, well, that's what we're there for."

Sometimes Nick's sensitivity shows when he least expects it. Take the first time he heard the recording of "True to Your Heart."

"When they sent us the tape to hear at home, I was almost in tears listening to it," Nick remembers.

A great-looking guy who is man enough to cry. Sounds almost too good to be true!

Nick is certainly making a lot more money these days than he did when he was working as a delivery boy for a Chinese restaurant. But if you think Nick's living large with big cars and fancy apartments, you're wrong. Like most Scorpios, money means very little to Nick.

Nick just got his own apartment in New York City, and in his own words, the place is "small and very modest. But it's home." Actually, Nick thinks it's kind of ironic the way fans think he lives the rock star life.

"People sometimes think that if you're a recording artist, everything is so easy. Like if you have a song on the radio, you must drive a Ferrari, have millions of dollars, and everything's beautiful and great. And there *are* a lot of great things about it, don't get me wrong. But there are struggles, too. The traveling is awfully hard. You go from one city to the next, every day. And there's missing your family, too. Still, we have a good time, and it hardly seems like work."

Are You the Girl for Nick?

Run off to your dentist. Hurry! You've got to get those teeth polished pearly white. Because when it comes to women, Nick says the first thing that attracts him is "a great smile."

Okay, that's easy, right? Well, everything about being Nick's lady wouldn't be quite so simple. Nick says that his girlfriend would have to be very secure. She'd have to be the kind of woman who could watch girls scream and blow kisses at her man, and still know he was hers and hers alone.

Believe it or not, Nick likes a little spice in his relationships. No, he doesn't mean he wants a relationship with one of the Spice Girls. He means he looks forward to someday finding a girlfriend who can hold her own in a heated discussion.

"I kind of like headstrong women," Nick

says. "I like to deal with adversity and have a struggle every now and then."

And now for the big question: Would Nick date a fan?

Good news—you betcha he would!

"I consider our fans our friends. So why not date a friend?" he says.

Why not indeed!

Fifty Fab Facts

We've piled together 50 important facts every 98 Degrees fan needs to know. Now you've got them all at your fingertips!

Did you know . . .
1. Jeff has two tattoos—one on his arm, which is the 98 Degrees logo, and one on his chest, which says "heaven" and "good luck" in Japanese.
2. Nick has thought about being a singer since elementary school!
3. Drew hates the nickname Andy. "No one has ever called me that and no one ever will!" he insists.
4. The first time Justin ever drove a car he was just nine years old!

5. Call Justin "Mr. Current Events." His favorite TV shows are the news magazines *20/20* and *60 Minutes*.

6. Jeff's favorite ice cream flavors are cookie dough and mint chocolate chip.

7. Drew's ex-girlfriend, Debbie, was one of the models picked to appear in "Was It Something I Didn't Say?"

8. Drew is a junk food junkie! (His faves are donuts!)

9. Justin's favorite actor is Robert DeNiro.

10. At 180 pounds, Nick is the heaviest member of 98 degrees (but it's all muscle!)

11. Jeff's favorite movie is *The Shawshank Redemption*.

12. Justin's nickname is Droopy.

13. Nick's nickname is Hollywood a.k.a. Slider.

14. Jeff's nickname is Sugar. (How sweet!)

15. Drew's nickname is Sprout.

16. Drew says the person he most admires is his dad.

17. Drew's dream car is a BMW M3.

18. Jeff calls working with Stevie Wonder "the biggest adrenaline rush ever!"

19. Nick's favorite color is red.

20. Jeff's favorite colors are orange and blue.
21. Justin's favorite color is blue.
22. Drew's favorite color is navy blue.
23. At 5'6", Drew is the shortest member of the group.
24. Jeff loves to chow down on steak and seafood. (Surf and turf, anyone?!)
25. Justin recently dyed his hair blond.
26. Justin is the only member of 98 Degrees without a tattoo. He says he hasn't found anything he'd like to have on his body forever.
27. Drew has one earring—a single hoop in his left ear.
28. Jeff's least favorite job ever was working as a nightclub security guard. "It was pretty dangerous," he admits.
29. Justin loves sunglasses. Fans send him pairs from all over the world!
30. Nick's favorite candy is the Kit Kat chocolate bar.
31. Jeff's dream car is a Ferrari.
32. Drew's favorite drink is orange juice.
33. Drew and Nick have matching arm band tattoos.
34. Nick plays the saxophone.

35. Drew's favorite song is "Purple Rain" by the Artist Formerly Known as Prince.

36. Justin thinks the biggest turn-off is girls who smoke cigarettes.

37. Nick's favorite actress is Michelle Pfeiffer.

38. Drew's hobbies are waterskiing and snowboarding.

39. Justin's goal is "to be a superstar who makes a difference."

40. Jeff's favorite music group is Boyz II Men.

41. Jeff compared getting his tattoos to "being bitten by loads of mosquitoes."

42. Nick's favorite song is "Cherish the Day" by Sade.

43. Jeff had to take his driving test twice before he passed it.

44. Nick is afraid of sharks.

45. Jeff's favorite song off the 98 Degrees album is "Heaven's Missing An Angel" because it reminds him of his grandmother, who died the day it was recorded.

46. Nick's most prized possessions are his CDs and tapes, and his stereo.

47. Drew finds dirty nails and bad breath a turn-off. (Who doesn't?)

48. Justin loves to sing in front of the mirror. (Well, who wouldn't want to look at that adorable face?!)

49. Nick says the most embarrassing thing that ever happened to him was when his overalls came unhooked during a concert in front of 3,000 cheerleaders.

50. 98 Degrees once had a gig scheduled in a bar in England. Only seven people showed, but the guys played their hearts out anyway!

Lights . . . Camera . . . Action!

When someone says the name 98 Degrees, you automatically think of music, right? But do you ever think of Jeff, Nick, Drew, and Justin as actors? Maybe you should.

Believe it or not, Justin, Jeff, Nick, and Drew *are* professional actors. Every time they make a video they are required to do the same things actors do—feel the emotions of the words, and relay those feelings to the audience. The only difference is the 98 Degrees guys get their words from song lyrics instead of lines in a script.

So which do the guys prefer—singing live or acting out a song in front of a camera? Well, let's just say that the guys have never felt quite as comfortable on a sound stage as they do on a concert stage. And that makes sense. Jeff, Justin, Nick, and Drew have been singing since they were kids. But before the guys filmed the video for "Invisible Man," the only guy in the group who'd ever done any professional acting on film was Jeff. And that was only in TV commercials. (The others had been in school plays, but that was about it).

So when it came time to make their first video, the guys were just a little worried. Could they pull it off? Could they perform in front of a camera and look professional?

It probably would have been easier for 98 Degrees to make a concert footage video their first time out. Performing is so comfortable for them. But taking the easy way out is not the 98 Degrees way. Besides, they wanted their video for "Invisible Man" to fit in with the meaning behind the song.

" 'Invisible Man' is about a guy who's in love with a girl and she's with somebody else and pretty much doesn't know he exists," Nick explains. "It's kinda about the frustration of being in love with someone who has no interest in you and doesn't give you any kind of feelings in return."

The boys wanted to make sure that the video depicted the loneliness, frustration, and alienation that the song talked about. So they stayed involved in every step of the preparation for the video. They worked with stylists to pick out their outfits, and made sure the hairstylists and make-up artists did not alter their individual looks.

Most importantly, the guys expressed their concern that a Hollywood sound stage could not properly convey the feelings in the song. A location scout was dispatched to find a more suitable location. He searched around until he found the perfect place to film the video—an empty abandoned chemical factory in Long Island City, New York.

When the guys first arrived on the set, they were thrilled with the spot the scout had found. The factory was perfect! Now they knew the video was going to be exactly what they had pictured.

"Our adrenaline was really flowing!" Justin recalls. "It was amazing, too, that production crew and the whole big extravaganza was put together all for us. That was the first realization that, wow, we're really about to jump into this business. It was a blast!"

Making the video may have been a blast, but it was also hard work. The guys had to learn all new skills. For starters, musical artists don't sing live when they make videos. They lip synch to already recorded music. That's something 98 Degrees wasn't used to doing. They always sing live in concert! The guys also had to practice showing their emotions on their faces and through their body movements, and not just with their voices. And they had to get used to calling up those emotions time and again because some scenes had to be shot several times. Giving a convincing performance over and over wasn't easy. But the guys mastered it.

"It's about feeling the music and listening to the lyrics," Jeff explains.

"When you have great lyrics, it's easy," Justin agrees. "You just go with your emotions."

The guys spent several days in that dank,

wet factory. For each minute of the final video, they worked about five and a half hours. But in the end, all that hard work paid off—big time! The video for "Invisible Man" got a lot of play on MTV and other video music channels. It introduced 98 Degrees to kids who may not have heard the single on the radio, and helped the song shoot its way into the gold zone!

Before long, fans were clamoring for another video. And you know there's nothing 98 Degrees would rather do than please their fans. So, soon after they'd finished shooting "Invisible Man," the guys went back in front of the cameras to shoot the video for "Was It Something I Didn't Say," the second single from *98 Degrees*.

Once again, the guys wanted a video that would reflect the emotions behind the song—this time about a guy who wonders why his girlfriend has left him. So Drew, Justin, Jeff, and Nick worked closely with director Darren Grant to come up with a concept they felt comfortable with. What they finally agreed on was having each member of the group paired with a beautiful girl who would play his ex. Then the guys would try to work their way through a twisting maze.

A giant, dark maze was constructed on a North Hollywood sound stage. 98 Degrees sang and danced together for the song's chorus scenes. Then they each performed separately. It was exhausting and the lights were hot. ("I think we're approaching 98 Degrees," Nick joked with one reporter.) But the guys kept their good humor, made several stops at the food table, and just kept at it.

"You just have to keep your energy up," Drew says of making the video. "You don't want to be doing anything else, but what you're doing is really tiring."

Nick especially liked the individual work each guy did on the "Was It Something I Didn't Say" video. "We all get to express the song in our own individual way. That's cool!" he exclaims.

Well, if the making of the "Was It Something I Didn't Say" video was cool, filming the "Because Of You" video was downright chilly! That's because it was shot high up on top of the windy Golden Gate Bridge in San Francisco.

"We were very afraid," Drew says of the filming. "But the director [Wayne Isham] had a great idea, and it was a beautiful location."

Jeff agreed that the Golden Gate Bridge location shoot was great for the video, but it was hard on him. "I'm definitely afraid of heights," he explains shyly.

The other group members were aware of Jeff's phobia and they rallied behind him, holding on to him when he was most nervous.

"At one point I was afraid Jeff was going to pull me off [the bridge]," Nick jokes.

But no one fell and the shoot went without a hitch.

"Because Of You" became a regularly requested video on MTV, and that led to the guys' guest appearance on the video channel's *Total Request Live* show. Their appearance on the show was proof positive that 98 Degrees had arrived. Only the top acts are invited to guest on that show! MTV confirmed their love of the 98 Degrees sound when they invited the guys to help ring in 1999 as musical guests on the *MTV New Years Live* celebration.

Perhaps the most exciting video 98 Degrees has ever made was the one for "True To Your Heart." The guys got to meet one of their idols, Stevie Wonder, for the very first time while shooting that one.

By now you are probably asking yourself, "How could that be? After all, the song 'True To Your Heart' was recorded before the video was made. Didn't the guys meet Stevie then?"

The answer to your question is no.

"We didn't get to record ['True To Your Heart'] with [Stevie Wonder] because our schedules were conflicting," Jeff explained to *Tiger Beat* magazine. "We went and laid down our part . . . and Stevie came in and sang [later].

"But we did get to meet him at the video shoot," Jeff continued. "He invited us to come into his trailer and we kind of had an on-the-spot jam session with him. For us, it was surreal almost. This is somebody who you idolized for so long, and you're sitting there with him."

The guys hung out with Stevie in his trailer for more than 20 minutes, singing songs like "In The Still Of The Night." They talked about their favorite groups like Boyz II Men and Take 6, as well as other groups whose music the guys and Stevie mutually enjoy.

According to Nick, Stevie Wonder told the guys that he loved their music. And, since 98 Degrees are never the type of guys to pass up an opportunity like that, they volunteered to sing back up for Stevie whenever he asked. So don't be surprised if you hear Stevie Wonder and 98 Degrees together again sometime in the future.

The guys later met up with Stevie again when they all performed "True To Your Heart" on *The Tonight Show with Jay Leno*.

"*The Tonight Show* was a huge thing!" Jeff told *Teen Machine*. "That's probably one of the biggest things we could ever do as a group. Not only were we there as a group, we were there with Stevie Wonder, performing a Disney song! It was very important for us."

After shooting their videos, 98 Degrees felt like pros. They knew all the ins and outs of bringing their songs to life on film. But video acting is not quite like acting on TV or in the movies. When you make a video, you don't have to talk (hey, you don't even have to actually *sing*). Acting on a TV sitcom with real actors is a different kind of challenge. And you know how the guys in 98 Degrees love a challenge. So, when their manager suggested they guest star on NBC's teen sitcom, *City Guys*, the 98 Degrees guys jumped at the opportunity.

Justin, Nick, Drew, and Jeff played themselves on *City Guys*. But that really didn't make things any easier. Nick admitted to *Teen Beat* that he was kind of nervous about saying his lines on the show.

"These people do it every day," he said of the *City Guys* actors. "Then we tried to come in and be normal. I kept asking myself, 'You're playing yourself, how hard can that really be?' But it is. It's a different scenario. And it is different than being in front of the cameras for a video or something. It's a different experience. . . . It kind of makes you appreciate movie actors because they're able to set up a character and at the same time they're having to start and stop. It's been an experience."

According to Drew, acting is much harder than singing in front of a live audience. "You can interact with the audience and you have something to feed off of," he explains. "You can grab hands and stuff. Otherwise you've just got this camera here, and it's not giving anything back to you."

"It's more staged and restricted an atmosphere than it is in a real concert," Jeff told *Superteen* magazine. "In a real concert, you can be spontaneous and do whatever you want."

Right now, 98 Degrees figure they'd be best off focusing on the music. "I don't think any of us are ready for acting at this point," Drew says. "I mean I'm sure we could do it if we took some classes in it and got schooled in it. But I think as of now, our best foot is 98 Degrees, and singing as a group. So we're gonna stick with that one."

Notice Drew made sure to add the words "at this point" to that statement. That's because all of the guys say that they would like to eventually branch off into acting someday as a group, if the right project came along. And with the success of the Spice Girls' *Spice World*, movie execs may just feel the time is right for another musical group to take their talents to the big screen.

Hello, Hollywood? Are you listening? Have we got a group for you!

What's Your Favorite Number?

What's your favorite number? It's got to be 98 of course! But there are other numbers you might appreciate, like 3, 4, or 5. That's because those are the numerological readings of the guys in 98 Degrees.

Numerology is a science that has been around since the times of the ancient Babylonians. Here's how it works:

According to numerology, everybody's personality falls into one of nine types. What type you fit into is determined by counting up the letters in your name.

Take Nick for instance. He may be your number one guy, a perfect 10, but in numerology, he's a five.

How did we get that? Easy! First we wrote

out all the letters in his full name (nicknames won't give you an accurate numerological reading). Then we matched the
letters with the numbers on this chart.

1	2	3	4	5	6	7	8	9
A	B	C	D	E	F	G	H	I
J	K	L	M	N	O	P	Q	R
S	T	U	V	W	X	Y	Z	

NICHOLAS SCOTT LACHEY
59386311 13622 313857

We added up all the numbers in Nick's
name and got a total of 77. But we weren't
finished yet. We then added the two sevens
in 77 together, and got a sum of 14. Then,
because numerology only works with single
digits, we added the 1 and the 4, and got a
sum of 5.

We did the same thing for the other guys
in the group. Here's what we discovered:
Andrew John Lachey is a 4. Justin Paul
Jeffre is a 4, also. Jeffrey Brandon Timmons
is a definite 3.
If you want to know what threes, fours,

and fives are like, and how *you* match up with your favorite hottie from 98 Degrees, add up the numbers in your name, and read on!

Ones are natural born leaders. They are extremely well organized, and like to tackle projects on their own because they love the spotlight. On the downside, ones can be ruthless. They need to learn to share the glory. Ones get along well with twos and sixes.

Twos are quiet and reserved. They make great diplomats because they take great care to try and understand both sides of any issue. Twos are very sensitive to criticism and need to develop a thicker skin. Twos mesh well with other twos, sevens, and eights.

Threes like Jeff are dynamic. People are just naturally drawn to them. (Just ask any girl who has written Jeff's name all over her notebook, or screamed to get his attention at a concert.) Threes are often trend-setters and leaders, which may explain why Jeff took it upon himself to start the band that eventually became known as 98 Degrees. Threes are fun loving, but they have sharp tongues and don't always realize that their jokes can hurt other's feelings. Even Jeff has to admit that in an interview situation he is the one who is sure to make a joke and wind up sticking his foot in his mouth. Threes get along well with fours and fives—which just happen to be the other members of 98 Degrees!

Fours like Drew and Justin take responsibility very seriously. Drew showed this trait way back in elementary school when he made sure he only sat where he could see and pay attention to the teacher. He later went on to become an emergency medical technician—a job in which you have to be extremely responsible since people's lives are on the line.

Fours are witty and entertaining. Justin fits that description to a T. Drew calls him the "party animal of the group." But like most fours, it's dangerous to argue with Justin. If he disagrees with you he won't hold back on the truth just to spare your feelings. "If you want the truth, go to Justin and you'll get it," Nick says. "He always tells you what he's thinking."

Fours are very compatible with twos, threes, and eights.

Fives are daredevils. They thrive on action and excitement. There's nothing more frightening to a five than boredom! So, being a five, Nick is always looking for a little adventure. (And boy, has he found it. With all their traveling, meeting fans, filming, and videos, being a member of 98 Degrees is, in itself, one big adventure!) Even Nick's favorite movie, *Die Hard*, is a real action thriller.

When Nick plays football (or any other game for that matter), watch out—like most fives, Nick really plays to win.

But don't let his bravado fool you. Fives have a sensitive side, and the girl who finally captures Nick's heart will find herself side by side with a real flowers and candy kind of sweetheart. But fives have to be careful— they tend to spend their money as fast as they earn it. And if 98 Degrees keeps going the way they have been, Nick will have plenty of dough to spend!

Sixes are kind, even tempered, and eager to help. They always look for the good in people, and while that can be a wonderful trait, it can also be dangerous. It makes them easy targets for people. Fives get along with twos, threes, and sevens.

Sevens have great eyes for spotting the latest and greatest things on the horizon. (Was it a seven who first played "Invisible Man" for you?) Sevens aren't just pop culture watchers. They are also very deep thinkers who tend to love heavy philosophical discussions. But when a seven is in deep-thinking mode, forget about changing the subject. She'll insist in talking things through for hours on end. Sevens get along well with fours, other sevens, eights, and nines.

Eights are highly disciplined people with intense powers of concentration. Those traits are important ingredients in any success recipe, so when they go for the gold, eights grab it every time. Eights never forget a kindness, but beware: they never forgive an injustice either. Forgive and forget is just not in an eight's vocabulary! Twos, fours, sixes, sevens, and nines go well with eights.

Nines are concerned with the well-being of Earth and everything that lives on it. They are the ones who save the whales, feed the children, and house the homeless. And that's a beautiful thing! We need nines. But the problem is, nines are often so busy helping the whole world that they neglect the people closest to them—their family and friends. Nines are extremely mercurial—happy one minute and crying the next. Nines are great matches for fours, sevens, and eights.

Quickie Questions and Snappy Comebacks!

Every day somebody somewhere is sticking a microphone in Justin's, Jeff's, Nick's, and Drew's faces, and asking them very personal questions. But the guys don't mind; they know it's all part of the job. The problem is, the reporters all seem to ask the exact same things. So, we're about to make the reporter's jobs really, really easy. Here, in their own words, are 98 Degrees' answers to their most frequently asked questions.

Q. How hot is 98 Degrees?
Drew: Scorching. It's heat, passion, love, and all that good stuff.
Nick: Hot as hell!

Jeff: Burning hot!
Justin: Body temperature.

Q. Who has the sloppiest hotel room?
Justin: Jeff.
Jeff: Justin.
Drew: Justin or Jeff.
Nick: Justin.

Q. What's your favorite pick-up line?
Nick: "Hi. My name is Nick."
Jeff: There's always, "Hi. How would you like to be in the next 98 Degrees video?"

Q. Do you guys ever fight?
Nick: We just ignore Drew's opinion and everything's fine.
Drew: We just ignore Nick, period.
(FYI: They were just joking. They're over that sib rivalry thing, honest!)

Q. When did you realize you were a star?

Drew: The first time [we traveled] in an actual real live tour bus.

Jeff: Yeah! We've got a driver now, so watch out!

Nick: We're movin' up, baby!

Q. What did it feel like to film the "Because Of You" video on top of the Golden Gate Bridge?

Drew: Windy.

Justin: A little chilly.

Jeff: Being on top of the bridge was almost surreal.

Nick: Scary. Very scary. And very, very exciting!

Q. Would you date a fan?

Justin: Yes!!!

Jeff: Yes.

Drew: I would have to know her a little first.

Nick: Sure.

Q. If you had the chance to become an invisible man, what would you do?

Jeff: Spy on a pretty girl.
Drew: Spy on my ex-girlfriend.
Nick: Visit the Dallas Cowboys Cheer-
leaders.
Justin: Steal from the rich and give to the
poor!

Jeff City for a previous t…
Drew: Slip on some comfortable…
Nick: Visit the Eyebrows Chapter…
leaders.
Justin: Heal from the soul, and give to the
poor.

The Ultimate 98 Degrees Trivia Test

Okay, we know you cherish 98 Degrees. To you, they're everything! But how much do you really know about Nick, Jeff, Justin, and Drew?

These trivia questions will help you find out whether you have 98 Degrees fever or not. Some will be pretty easy for you—the answers are hidden somewhere in this book. But others will be "The Hardest Thing"! In fact, we're not even sure the boys themselves know all these facts about each other.

Are you ready? Okay, let the quiz begin!

1. True or false: 98 Degrees is the first all-white band to be signed to the Motown label.

2. What is 98 Degrees Inc.?
3. Where did Drew go to high school?
4. During interviews, which 98 Degrees guy usually puts his foot in his mouth?
5. What was the group's debut single?
6. Which two teams played in the NBA finals game at which 98 Degrees sang the national anthem?
7. How high did "Invisible Man" go on the *Billboard* singles charts?
8. Which member of the group once worked as an emergency medical technician in Brooklyn?
9. What was the first song recorded for *98 Degrees and Rising*?
10. Of which song on *98 Degrees and Rising* has Drew said, "I get goosebumps every time I hear it"?
11. 98 Degrees joined a group of singers and athletes to record "We're All In This Together." What charitable organization did the proceeds from the single go to?
12. Is there a Play Station on the 98 Degrees tour bus?
13. Where was the video for "Invisible Man" shot?

14. Which 98 Degrees hottie attended Miami University in Ohio?

15. True or false: One of Drew's nicknames is Radar, based on the short character on TV's M*A*S*H.

16. What two instruments does Jeff play?

17. What size baseball cap does Drew wear?

18. "True To Your Heart" appears on what two albums?

19. What song did 98 Degrees perform on *City Guys?*

20. On which float did 98 Degrees ride in the 1998 Macy's Thanksgiving Day Parade?

21. What song did the guys perform on *The Tonight Show?*

22. How many record labels originally approached 98 Degrees?

23. *98 Degrees and Rising* debuted at what number on the Canadian album charts?

24. What was Justin's major in college?

25. True or false: Jeff is a professional actor.

26. "Fly With Me" samples what ABBA tune?

27. What country star originally made a hit of "I Do (Cherish You)"?

28. Who has the Japanese symbols for heaven and good luck tattooed on his chest?

29. Which 98 Degree hottie has the middle name Scott?

30. Finish this lyric from "Because Of You." "I said baby I should have known by now Should have been right there whenever _____."

31. On December 1, 1998, 98 Degrees made their first live appearance on what MTV show?

32. What kind of camps did 98 Degrees visit on their 1998 summer U.S. tour?

33. Who is the founding member of 98 Degrees?

34. Which member of 98 Degrees loves Yoo Hoo chocolate drink?

35. What is Justin's natural hair color?

36. Which 98 Degrees member started Just Us?

37. The 98 Degrees Foundation benefits what type of charities?

38. True or false: Nick has a daughter.

39. What magazine called 98 Degrees "the most elegant of the boy bands"?

40. 98 Degrees were on the cover of the premiere issue of what magazine?

41. Who are Cate and John?
42. What is Justin's favorite football team?
43. True or false: Drew was against signing with Motown.
44. What song from 98 Degrees and Rising was on the group's original demo tape?
45. The video for "Because Of You" was shot on the top of what bridge?
46. Which 98 Degrees guy winks at girls from the stage?
47. What was the first expensive item Justin bought after the group made it big?
48. What does Justin like best about being a musician?
49. Who is Paris D'Jon?
50. What kinds of songs does Justin consider the group's "strong point"?

Answers to the Ultimate 98 Degrees Trivia Test
  1. True
  2. The corporation that oversees the business aspects of the group
  3. The Cincinnati School for Creative and Performing Arts
  4. Jeff
  5. "Invisible Man"

6. The Chicago Bulls and the Utah Jazz
7. It reached number twelve.
8. Drew
9. "True To Your Heart"
10. "She's Out Of My Life"
11. The United Way
12. Of course!
13. Long Island City, N.Y.
14. Nick
15. True
16. Harmonica and trombone
17. Size 7
18. The *Mulan* soundtrack and *98 Degrees and Rising*
19. "I Do (Cherish You)"
20. The Planters Peanuts float
21. "True To Your Heart"
22. Three
23. #40
24. History
25. True. He appeared in a few commercials before joining 98 Degrees, including one for the Navy.
26. "Dancing Queen"
27. Mark Wills
28. Jeff
29. Nick

30. "You gave me love"
31. *Total Request*
32. Cheerleading camps
33. Jeff
34. Nick
35. Brown
36. Jeff
37. Children's charities
38. False, he has no children.
39. *Entertainment Weekly*
40. *Teen Celebrity*
41. Nick and Drew's parents
42. The Cincinnati Bengals
43. False. The decision was unanimous and quick!
44. "She's Out Of My Life"
45. The Golden Gate Bridge
46. Justin (The others say he's a BIG FLIRT!)
47. $300 sunglasses
48. The traveling
49. 98 Degrees' manager
50. Ballads

How Do You Measure Up?
Okay, here's where we separate the true 98 Degrees fans from the rest of the crowd!

Does your score "Heat It Up"—or should you just "Give It Up"?

To find out, add up all of your correct answers. Then check the chart.

40–50 correct: Whew! Is it getting hot in here? You've really got the 98 Degrees fever!

29–39 correct: Great score! It's "Because Of You" (and fans like you) that the guys keep on making music!

15–28 correct: Whoops! Your score is sinking. You'd better pop a 98 Degrees CD into your stereo and listen up if you want to stay "True To Your Heart" as a 98 Degrees fan!

0–14 correct: Oh no! You need help. But never fear. Just read the book again, you'll have that score on the rise in no time!

13

The 98 Degrees Discography

98 Degrees
Motown Records
July 29, 1997

1. **Intro** (0:38)
Written by: 98 Degrees and Bernard Grubman

2. **Come And Get It** (4:28)
Written by: Montell Jordan
Produced by: Montell Jordan

3. **Invisible Man** (4:41)
Written by: Dane DeViller, Sean Hosein, and Steve Kipner

Produced by: Dane DeViller and Sean Hosein

4. Take My Breath Away (4:31)
Written by: Steve Grissette and Maxx Frank
Produced by: Steve Grissette and Maxx Frank

5. Hand In Hand (5:18)
Written by: Mario Winans and Kenneth Hickson
Produced by: Mario Winans

6. Intermood (0:31)
Written by: 98 Degrees and Bernard Grubman

7. Dreaming (4:00)
Written by: Montell Jordan, Shep Crawford, and Professor Funk
Produced by: Montell Jordan, Shep Crawford, and Professor Funk

8. You Are Everything (2:50)
Written by: Thom Bell and Linda Creed
Produced by: Mario Winans

9. **Heaven's Missing An Angel** (4:42)
Written by: Christopher A. Stewart, Sean K.
Hall, Sam Salter, and Tab
Produced by: Tricky and Sean

10. **I Wasn't Over You** (4:20)
Written by: Christopher A. Stewart, Sean K.
Hall, and Tab
Produced by: Tricky and Sean

11. **Completely** (4:05)
Written by: 98 Degrees and Bernard Grubman

12. **Don't Stop The Love** (4:31)
Written by: Christopher A. Stewart, Sean K.
Hall, and Robin Thicke
Produced by: Tricky and Sean

13. **I Wanna Love You** (4:00)
Written by: Kenny Greene, Rashad Smith,
and Armando Colon
Produced by: Rashad Smith

98 Degrees (Reissue)
Motown Records
March 10, 1998

1. **Intro** (0:38)
Written by: 98 Degrees and Bernard Grubman

2. **Come And Get It** (4:28)
Written by: Montell Jordan
Produced by: Montell Jordan

3. **Invisible Man** (4:41)
Written by: Dane DeViller, Sean Hosein, and Steve Kipner
Produced by: Dane DeViller and Sean Hosein

4. **Was It Something I Didn't Say** (5:02)
Written by: Diane Warren
Produced by: Darryl Simmons

5. **Take My Breath Away** (4:31)
Written by: Steve Grissette and Maxx Frank
Produced by: Steve Grissette and Maxx Frank

6. **Hand In Hand** (5:18)
Written by: Mario Winans and Kenneth Hickson
Produced by: Mario Winans

7. **Intermood** (0:31)
Written by: 98 Degrees and Bernard Grubman

8. **Dreaming** (4:00)
Written by: Montell Jordan, Shep Crawford, and Professor Funk
Produced by: Montell Jordan, Shep Crawford, and Professor Funk

9. **Heaven's Missing An Angel** (4:42)
Written by: Christopher A. Stewart, Sean K. Hall, Sam Salter, and Tab
Produced by: Tricky and Sean

10. **I Wasn't Over You** (4:20)
Written by: Christopher A. Stewart, Sean K. Hall, and Tab
Produced by: Tricky and Sean

11. **Completely** (4:05)
Written by: 98 Degrees and Bernard Grubman

12. **Don't Stop The Love** (4:31)
Written by: Christopher A. Stewart, Sean K. Hall, and Robin Thicke
Produced by: Tricky and Sean

13. **I Wanna Love You** (4:00)
Written by: Kenny Greene, Rashad Smith, and Armando Colon
Produced by: Rashad Smith

98 Degrees and Rising
Motown Records
October 27, 1998
Certified Gold, December, 1998

1. **Intro** (0:41)
Produced by: 98 Degrees

2. **Heat It Up** (4:15)
Written by: 98 Degrees, Mark Adams, Steve Arrington, Mark Hicks, Thomas Lockett, Raymond Turner, Daniel Webster, and Starleana Taylor
Produced by: Poke and Tone
Vocals Produced and Arranged by: 98 Degrees

3. **If She Only Knew** (4:27)
Written by: Chris Farren and Gordon Chambers

Produced by: Dane DeViller and Sean Hosein
Co-Produced by: 98 Degrees

4. I Do (Cherish You) (3:45)
Written by: Keith Stegall and Dan Hill
Produced by: Keith Thomas

5. Fly With Me (3:49)
Written by: 98 Degrees, S.P. Michel, Jerry Duplessis, Stig Anderson, Bjoern Ulvaeus, and Benny Anderson
Produced by: Pras Michel
Co-Produced by: Jerry "Wonder" Duplessis
Vocals Produced and Arranged by: 98 Degrees

6. Still (4:00)
Written by: 98 Degrees, Dane DeViller, and Sean Hosein
Produced by: Dane Deviller and Sean Hosein
Co-Produced by: 98 Degrees

7. Because Of You (4:58)
Written by: Anders Bagge, Arntor Birgisson, Christian Karlsson, and Patrick Tucker
Produced by: Bag, Bloodshy, and Arntor

8. Give It Up (Interlude) (1:31)
Written by: 98 Degrees
Produced by: 98 Degrees

9. Do You Wanna Dance (4:14)
Written by: 98 Degrees, Jean Claude Olivier, Samuel Barnes, Robert Bell, James Taylor, George Brown, Ronald Bell, Charles Smith, Robert Mickens, and Eumir Deodato
Produced by: Poke and Tone
Vocals Produced and Arranged by: 98 Degrees

10. True To Your Heart (4:15)
Written by: Matthew Wilder and David Zippel
Produced and Arranged by: Matthew Wilder

11. To Me You're Everything (4:09)
Written by: Anders Bagge, Laila Bagge, Jocelyn Gueridon Mathieux, Maurice White, Eduardo Del-Barrio, and Verdine White
Produced by: Bag

12. The Hardest Thing (4:34)
Written by: Steve Kipner and David Frank

Produced and Arranged by: David Frank
and Steve Kipner
Additional Production by: 98 Degrees

13. **She's Out Of My Life** (3:07)
Written by: Tom Bahler
Produced by: 98 Degrees
Co-Produced by: Devon Biere

Singles

"Invisible Man"
June 24, 1997
#12 *Billboard* Hot 100
Certified Gold on October 22, 1997

"Because of You"
September 15, 1998
#3 on *Billboard* Hot 100
Certified Gold on October 26, 1998
Certified Platinum on December 3, 1998

Compilations

NFL Jams
October 20, 1998
"We're All In This Together"

98 Degrees was part of a singing ensemble of R&B artists and NFL Players to record this song, which celebrates the NFL's 25-year relationship with the United Way.

Bop Boys
November 1998
"Invisible Man"

Catch 98 Degrees with a Net (Address)

Are you wondering what songs 98 Degrees sang in their latest Malaysian concert? How about how well their album is doing on the Canadian charts? Maybe you just want to talk to other girls who think Drew's baseball hats are the greatest fashion statement ever. If there's anything you want to know about 98 Degrees, the best place to go (besides inside the pages of this book) is the internet.

There are so many Web sites devoted to 98 Degrees these days that it would take you weeks to go through them all. But what better way to spend your time than looking at hot new pictures of Nick, Drew, Jeff, and

Justin, reading about their likes and loves, and chatting with others about the meanings of their songs?!

Perhaps the best place to start is the official 98 Degrees Web site:

www.98degrees.com

That site will give you news and schedule updates as well as information that comes straight from the guys. You can also enter your e-mail address and receive news from 98 Degrees approximately once every two weeks.

There's also official 98 Degrees information coming from the Motown site, 98 Degrees-No Flash. The site is located at:

www.motown40.com/history/archives/0_9/ 98/index_alt.html

After you've checked out the official sites, you can move onto the pages set up by fans like you, from all over the world. Here are just a few Web site addies no 98 Degrees fan should be without. Take your time, and go through them all. But as always, when you are on the internet, play it smart. Feel free to e-mail other 98 Degrees fanatics! But never give out your real name, phone number, or address. And never, *ever* agree to an in-person meeting with anyone you meet over the internet.

FYI: Web sites come and go faster than you can say "megabyte"! So some of these may no longer be available by the time you check them out. Of course, on the other hand, new ones are popping up all the time!

98 Degrees and Rising:
www.geocities.com/SunsetStrip/Frontrow/
4750/contents.html

98 Hearts:
www.geocities.com/SunsetStrip/
Amphitheatre/5088/intro.html

98 Degrees' Heaven:
www.geocities.com/Vienna/Strasse/8911/
index.html

Warm and Smooth Completely 98 Degrees:
www.geocities.com/Paris/Metro/4383

Before They Were Famous:
tinpan.fortunecity.com/blondie/195/
famous.html

98 Degrees Kingdom:
www.geocities.com/Hollywood/screen/
4320

Prepare to Get Burned by 98 Degrees:
members.tripod.com/~GetBurned/
index.html

The Singapore 98 Degrees Site:
www.geocities.com/soho/studios/9234

98 Degrees Centre:
www.geocities.com/Broadway/Stage/4385

Platinum Plus:
www.geocities.com/SunsetStrip/Arena/
1580

Hot 98:
www.geocities.com/Hollywood/Boulevard/
8987

The First Unofficial 98 Degrees Webring:
www.webring.org/cgi-bin/webring?ring=
hot98degrees;list

If you're not plugged into the net yet, don't despair. You can still reach 98 Degrees. Try writing them at Motown:

> 98 Degrees
> c/o Motown Record Company, LP
> 825 Eighth Ave.
> New York, NY 10019
> USA

You can also call the official 98 Degrees toll-free fan hot line at 877-980-9898. (Be sure to get your parents' permission.) That's where you'll get information on how to join the Official 98 Degrees Fan Club. Fan Club members pay a fee and in return receive a newsletter, a membership card, a poster, an autographed photo, stickers, and a stick-on tattoo. There are also contests just for official fan club members.

Whether you keep up with the guys on the net, through the mail or by phone, isn't it nice to know that no matter where you go it's always 98 Degrees?!

About the Author

Nancy E. Krulik is a freelance writer who has previously written biographies of pop music phenoms Taylor Hanson, Isaac Hanson, and New Kids on the Block. She is also the author of the best-selling *Leonardo DiCaprio: A Biography,* and the trivia books *Pop Quiz* and *Pop Quiz: Leonardo DiCaprio.* Nancy's favorite hobby is trying to spot music sensations on the rise, and 98 Degrees definitely qualifies! She lives in Manhattan with her husband, composer Daniel Burwasser, and their two children.

Five

The members of Five, Britain's hot new boy band, met last year at a London talent search and things "just clicked." Since that fateful day, these lovable lads—Rich, Sean, Scott, Abs, and J—have carried out a full-scale British Invasion of the U.S. pop scene with their edgy blend of soul, hip-hop, rap, and some serious attitude, creating a unique sound that blows the competition away.

With the complete 411 on these bright British stars, this book will leave you "Satisfied"!

By Matt Netter

Available now!

Published by Pocket Books

POCKET BOOKS

2087

THE HOTTEST STARS
THE BEST BIOGRAPHIES

☆ **Hanson: MMMBop to the Top** ☆
By Jill Mattthews

☆ **Hanson: The Ultimate Trivia Book!** ☆
By Matt Netter

☆ **Isaac Hanson: Totally Ike!** ☆
By Nancy Krulik

☆ **Taylor Hanson: Totally Taylor!** ☆
By Nancy Krulik

☆ **Zac Hanson: Totally Zac!** ☆
By Matt Netter

☆ **Jonathan Taylor Thomas:**
Totally JTT! ☆
By Michael-Anne Johns

☆ **Leonardo DiCaprio: A Biography** ☆
By Nancy Krulik

☆ **Will Power!**
A Biography of Will Smith ☆
By Jan Berenson

☆ **Prince William:**
The Boy Who Will Be King ☆
By Randi Reisfeld

Available from Archway Paperbacks
Published by Pocket Books